"Life's like a movie, write your own ending. Keep believing, keep pretending."

Jim Henson

Stake Your Claim:
The Four Ways Your Business Must
Win in the Wild West of the Web

Ian J. Garlic
Second Edition
First Printing - Hard Cover

Copyright © 2011 by Ian Garlic
All rights reserved. No part of this publication may be reproduced, stored in a retrieval system, or transmitted, in any form or by any means, electronic, mechanical, photocopying, recording, or otherwise, without the prior written permission of the publisher.

Ian Garlic
3586 Aloma Ave, Suite 12
Winter Park, FL 32792
iangarlic.com
USA

ISBN-13: 978-1492888406
ISBN-10: 1492888400

Printed in the United States of America

Design & Layout:
Jessica Curry Garlic

Illustrations:
Bianca Akhidime

Stake Your Claim:

The Four Ways Your Business Must Win in the WILD WEST of the Web

by Ian J. Garlic

Illustrations: Bianca Akhidime
Book Design: Jessica Curry

Thanks to my family, all of our great clients, our team at authenticWEB and to my amazing wife Jessica, without whom I still would be wandering trying to Stake My Claim.

PROLOGUE

Many fortunes are yet to be made on the internet. Even if you don't want to run an internet-based business, there are huge opportunities for your current real world business. This is especially true if you are a fixer. A fixer is a professional in a service-based industry who fixes things. Those things can be teeth, legal problems, bodies, cars, or any number of problems or items. Through a well designed internet presence a fixer can stake a claim on the web. Leveraging the power of the internet, the fixer (you) will generate a stream of business allowing you to focus on doing the things a fixer does best, fixing things.

Three years have passed since I wrote the first draft of Stake Your Claim. There have been many books written on internet marketing during the past three years, and technology has continued to change and evolve, but my original message has stayed the same. Only minor changes have been made to the initial draft.

Simplicity was the goal with this new draft. When I first wrote Stake Your Claim, I thought that people already knew the fundamentals that I have written in this latest draft. I thought, to make my book timeless, I would need to be ahead of the curve, a trendsetter. In actuality, I needed to tone the book down. Business owners still do not truly understand the philosophies and the fundamentals that make it possible to be found through search engines. It seems there is actually more misinformation on this subject than I initially realized.

I find it fascinating that search engines have not significantly changed over the past few years. Social media has changed, but search fundamentals are still the same. Google tried to create a different search engine that did not use links (one of the four pieces of internet capital), but Google failed. I am sure that there will be a technological shift, but for now it is not obvious what it will entail. So, it is safe to say, these pieces of internet capital are here to stay for a little while. From the many things you should learn for your business, this is my top advice. If you build on the four pieces of internet capital laid forth in this book, your stream of new clients will compound. You will have a successful business generated from online marketing no matter what type of fixing you do.

Table of Contents

Introduction	1
Stake Your Claim: The Story	4
Let's Set Out on Staking Your Claim	7
Your First Piece of Capital: Survey and Stake Your Claim	9
Your Second Piece of Capital: Develop Your Claim	11
Your Third Piece of Capital: Get the Town Pointing to You	13
Your Fourth Piece of Capital: Your Reputation	14
The Story Explained	16
Glossary	18
Four Keys to Winning in the Wild Frontier: Your Internet Capital	21
Your First Piece of Internet Capital: Survey and Stake Your Claim	22
Your Second Piece of Internet Capital: Links	24
Your Third Piece of Internet Capital: Your Content	27
Your Fourth Piece of Capital in the Virtual Frontier: Your Online Reputation	30
Where to Go From Here?	32

INTRODUCTION

The Who, How, & Why of This Book

Will you benefit from this book?

This book is for service professionals who would like to see their business expand by winning on the web. To do this there are four areas of the web, the compulsories, that must be understood. These compulsories are the Four Pieces of Internet Capital: your domain, your links, your content, and your online reputation. Anyone that is an expert in their field and provides services should memorize these four pieces of capital and how they work. Building upon them will soon become second nature and lay an incredible foundation for marketing your business on the internet.

While most of the techniques found in this book apply to every internet business, the descriptions here are specifically intended for those who are trying to find new and better clients and patients through the web.

I have used these techniques for the following service industries and been met with great success:

- Attorneys
- Dentists
- Photographers
- Financial Advisors
- Catering Companies
- Event Planners
- Writers
- Assisted Living Facilities
- Event Professionals
- Editors
- Publishers
- Auto Mechanics
- Entrepreneurs

So, why did I make up a story to teach this?

Well, first of all, it's fun. I firmly believe that you should inject fun into everything you do! Second of all, telling your story is an essential component for being successful on the web. What better way to convey the power of a story than with a story? Many of the professionals I have worked with do not remember the four pieces of internet capital, nor do they completely understand how they work. I hope the story I've included will help you understand and remember the essentials whether you have succeeded in applying them already or are just starting to use them in your business. We remember stories. Our brains operate in stories. This story is meant to give you the foundation to stake and build your claim with a great internet presence.

"My business is fine; I don't need a great internet presence"

Many professionals create an internet presence as an after thought. These professionals come scrambling to our internet marketing agency, authenticWEB, when their pipeline of new prospects drops off. I have had many encounters with professionals whose business dried up after major shifts happened in the decision making habits of their customers and clients. Then they scramble to get in the internet marketing game.

Referrals dry up and the professionals don't know why. In case you haven't noticed, the internet is growing. Everyone researches on the web; I mean everyone. From toilet paper to BMWs, from houses to potential spouses, it is being researched online! So, the referrals might happen, but most of these referrals will use the internet to research your business. If you don't have an internet presence, then they won't find you. Worse yet, they will find your competition. Eventually no internet presence means no business.

With information at our fingertips, search engines have changed the way people shop for everything, including your services! There are over one billion Facebook users alone, and that number is constantly growing. What makes you think your next client is not starting their search for your services on the web? It is a statistical improbability that your next client isn't on the web, searching for your services and researching you. Ignoring the web will not make it go away, and your business will suffer for it. I have worked with thirty year old law firms that now receive 70% of their business from the web only because they recognized and seized the opportunity available to them.

Think of it this way. When was the last time you made any decision without first checking the internet? Hiring a fixer is a huge decision, and most decisions are made using the internet.

"But I already have an SEO expert."

The principles in this book are just as essential to your business as the knowledge of basic accounting. Sure you have an accountant, but you need a basic understanding of money to communicate with them properly. Just as those basic cash-flow principles should guide you in your day to day business, the principles in this book will allow you to better communicate with your SEO expert and to develop strategies with them. The knowledge here can save you money, time, and lots of heartache. Trust me, I have dealt with many so-called SEO experts. For now, there is no CPA designation or licensing, and it all moves too fast for there to be one. There are some fantastic authorities out there, but there are many that barely know the basics, much less the advanced techniques based on the fundamentals laid forth in this book.

"Is this all I need to know to get more clients from the web?"

The knowledge in this book is a foundation. Your Four Pieces of Internet Capital are the compulsories. You will have success if you focus on these. In order to dominate the web you will need to learn much more. Reading this will give you the understanding and the tools to not only to do well but to learn more in order to create your web presence or to hire a great team to help you create it. After you have learned these basics, you can slowly add new techniques to this foundation to grow and evolve with the web. Even if you don't add more advanced techniques to the ones presented in this book, you can still attain a great level of success by applying these four basic principles.

"How am I going to make it work? I don't have time to do all of this."

If you don't have time, you should be making enough money to hire someone to do it for you. If you don't have the time AND no money, you need to make time. Marketing is what makes a business happen. Plain and simple. There is nothing more important than marketing your business and no more powerful tool to marketing it than the internet. There are many people setting out to stake their claim on the web. It is getting crowded, so the sooner you get started, the easier it will be.

Are you excited?
You should be.

It's time to head to the
Wild West of The Web
so that you can
Stake Your Claim!

Stake Your Claim: The Story

Now that we know our basics, let's take a trip. Imagine, if you will, that you are a fixer, dreaming of the riches of the Wild West of the Web.

You fix specific problems with your education and skills. You fix things when they are broken, whether it's a car, a contract, or a broken heart. You love to help others, and you love your craft.

You are also an adventurer. You don't want anyone to tell you what to do or which way to go with your business. Big Fixin' shops are mills, and they are everywhere in your busy city. You want to create your own lifestyle and work with the people that you like, fixing the problems you like to fix.

Sure, there is opportunity to work in big buildings, for big companies, and to work your way up to the top. But you knew that's not for you, so you started your own thing and ventured into business for yourself. You sold fixes. You started to advertise in the local paper, but there were so many fixers all around, and everyone you met had "their" fixer in the big city. You didn't want to sell out to advertising and become just another fixer with your face plastered on a bus bench. **You knew the way you fixed was special.**

Then you noticed something going on. You looked out there, to the Great Internet Frontier, The Wild West of the Web (WWW). You had seen people building empires in there. You had heard stories of dentists, lawyers, doctors, and other fixers becoming successful in the Wild West of the Web. Fixers just like you had come back to town with carts full of new riches, entire wagon trains parading through town and showing off despite any actual skills in fixing. You knew these people did not have your spirit or spunk. They did not have your integrity. You fix things the right way. They had not practiced the art of fixing, like you. You asked yourself, *How did they do it? How did they all become successful? How did they make it look so easy? Not all of the fixers that venture out there succeed. Why did they?*

You had also heard horrible stories of people venturing out into this Great Frontier, the Wild West of the Web. They set out with guides that claimed to be experts in the Wild West of the Web. These guides showed your fixer friends posters of their conquests and seemingly authentic maps to treasure with big X's on them. They made bold claims, such as, "I'm gonna make you rich because I know the Sheriff, and he makes everyone rich." These fixers had businesses just like your business. These fixers were smart just like you and had plenty of resources.

Then you saw these same fixers come back with no money. They strode back home feeling lost, with empty pockets, or worse, they did not come back to town at all. Some fixers just disappeared, swallowed up by the empty frontier. Some came back to work in the Big Mills.

You had also heard of this Sheriff. You heard that he is the one that runs the Wild West of the Web. He leads people to the right fixers and tries to keep out the bad guys, the Black Hats. The Sheriff is mysterious, but he seems to be everywhere in the Great Frontier, watching over it, keeping everyone in line.

You had heard of the Black Hats as well. You'd heard that they want to take shortcuts to gain riches in the Wild West of the Web. They want to outsmart the Sheriff. But you'd also heard that while the Black Hats may elude the Sheriff for a while, in the end, the Black Hats will get their due.

After considering all you had heard, you decided the Wild West of the Web is where you need to take your business. That is where I came in. I will be your guide into the Wild West of the Web. If you are ready, we will the hop next train heading there.

Let's set out on Staking Your Claim.

When the train heading toward the Wild West of the Web starts to move, I can sense your excitement. We start to pass lots of towns and see lots of opportunities for fixers like you. I see your eyes sparkling as you see people you know with huge (and growing bigger) businesses built on Main Street, in the busiest towns. Their stores are filled with the clients you would like to claim!

While we travel, I decide to tell you about the basics: First, I want to tell you about the Sheriff. Then as we explore, I will tell you about the four tools you need to win, your four pieces of capital in the Wild West of the Web, which we will refer to as the WWW.

The Sheriff of the Wild West of the Web wants everyone in town to play nicely. The Sheriff doesn't have time to scold people for not playing by the rules, so it's his way or the highway.

The Sheriff wants to see businesses succeed in the WWW. He collects their information and provides it to anyone looking to buy things or for answers in the WWW. In order to keep things straight and make sure everything runs smoothly in the WWW, the Sheriff has made rules for success and rules never to be broken. You need to understand the Sheriff's rules. Get caught breaking the rules, and you are out of his town.

There are Four Pieces of Capital you are going to need to develop to have a successful Fixin' Shop and keep in the Sheriff's good graces. Abide by his rules and develop your capital in the WWW, and I promise you will have a thriving, growing business. Here are the Four Pieces of Capital you need to develop in the Wild West of the Web:

1. Your Claim [Your Domain Names and URLs]
2. People pointing to your business/ Referrals [Your Links]
3. The rooms in your fixing shop [Your Content]
4. The talk of the town [Your Online Reputation]

The Sheriff's rules go like this. Make sure your claim is original and well kept. Make sure those answers are your answers. Don't pay people to talk about your shop without making sure they tell people you paid them.

Your First Piece of Capital: Survey and Stake Your Claim

Right when we get off the train some guys come running up. These shady looking characters tell you that they can get you front and center on Main Street, that you will be the biggest store. They say they can guarantee to make you number one. They say they know the Sheriff. Some of them are wearing those black hats you have heard about, and some have pretty badges that look like the Sheriff's badge.

Always remember this: There are no shortcuts without consequences down the road. There are no guarantees in the Wild West of the Web.

Let's get started by laying a good foundation:

The first thing you need to do in the Wild West of the Web is to find a plot of land. There are many pre-built businesses on very busy streets being leased out to fixers like you. To really succeed in our Great Frontier, to really lay a great foundation, you need your own piece of land. You don't want to spend a lot of time developing a storefront, telling people where you are, and getting regular customers only to lose it all one day. You might get evicted, or the Sheriff might shut the landlord down. The street might become deserted. The landlord might like your business so much that he increases the rent or even takes your Fixin' Shop for himself. You don't ever want to start all over.

That can easily happen if you don't build on your own land. It may be easier just to rent right now, but we have the resources to build you a nice place, and as you expand you will appreciate it.

So where do you start? Well, if you have a name for yourself out here, you can start where everyone knows you. Hang your business name out there. But most likely, the people in the new frontier won't be looking for you by name. If you don't have a name for yourself, you will want to be on a street where other fixers like you are located. People will find you more easily that way.

If you are not quite sure about the exact type of fixing that you will be doing, you will want to be somewhere that people are familiar with you, on a street that is general. Being very clear with your claim helps the Sheriff know what type of fixin' you are going to be doing.

Deciding where to initially stake your claim is a big consideration. If you change your address later on, you can re-point signs and let everyone know where you moved, but you still may lose some customers. You may also counteract much of the hard work you put into creating this foundation.

Once you have staked your claim, it is now time to start developing it.

Your Second Piece of Capital: Develop Your Claim

You have laid your claim in the Wild West of the Web. Now, you need to start setting up shop on your new property, letting people know what you fix and how you do it. You start by hanging your sign. Your sign gives an overview of the fixing from the front door. You then want to build different rooms where you can show off the different ways you can help people. You can have all types of Fixin' Rooms in your shop. If you fix teeth, you can have Fixin' Rooms for making teeth shiny, for replacing teeth, and for making new teeth. It's better to have lots of small rooms so potential clients feel like you have a Fixin' Room just for them. Still, it should all fit in with the idea of what you fix, the way you fix, and the sign on your front door. These rooms can even have their own little side doors, so your patrons feel comfortable walking in, getting exactly what they need fixed, and walking out. The amazing part about building all of these rooms is that you are building up your capital. Every room you build increases the value of your real estate.

You see a fixer just like you down the street. You admire his store and see that he has lots of patrons, so you think you will copy him. Slow down. You can't just set up the store exactly like another one down the street. The Sheriff in this town won't stand for that.

He wants your claim to be original, and he wants all of the residents and visitors coming to the Wild West of the Web to have a great and unique experience. You have to put your own spin on things. The more originality and creativity you put into your Fixin' Shop, the more people will remember it. The Sheriff likes originality and won't stand for knockoffs. Originality gives the visitors and residents of WWW many options and a great experience, which attracts even more people.

Develop as many rooms as possible. Redecorate them regularly and keep them up. This second piece of capital should constantly be in development.

Now that you have developed on your claim, let's make it more prominent.

Your Third Piece of Capital: Get The Town Pointing to You

You know referrals are the best source of income for fixers back home. Well, the same thing goes for the Wild West of the Web. Ask your friends, new and old, as well as other businesses, to talk about your business. You want to create remarkable rooms to get even strangers talking about your Fixin' Shop. As more people talk about it, the Sheriff will guide more people to your shop.

Don't pay people to refer to your shop unless they are very clear that it is a paid endorsement.

The Sheriff takes referrals very seriously, and if you try to play games you will get caught. The Sheriff is big time. He made the Wild West of the Web what it is today. Even some Big Money City Folk have tried to beat the Sheriff at his game, but he always catches them and kicks them out of town. No one has a deal with the Sheriff. NO ONE. Just play by his rules, and you will be fine.

What you need to do is stay on course. Build more rooms, do a great job, and give people a reason to talk about you. Help others promote their businesses. Get noticed by authoritative people and get them talking about you. If you keep being a part of the community and adding value, more people will refer to your shop. You shop will become more important, get more traffic, and you can afford to fix up your Fixin' Shop in even better ways, all while playing by the Sheriff's rules.

Now it's time to pay attention to what everyone else is saying about you and your shop. You want to monitor and respond to the conversation. If you get big enough, someone, somewhere will have something not nice to say.

Your Fourth Piece of Capital: Your Reputation

You want everyone to find The (Almost) World Famous Fixer's Fixin' Shop of Webstown. You have answers tailored to every possible client. You have signs up and business is booming. Then, suddenly everything stops. The phones stop ringing. People walk in, they talk about buying, but you never see them again. Your Fixes are just sitting on the shelves, alone in their rooms. No one wants you to fix anymore.

What happened? You have been so busy paying attention to building your shop that you never walked around town. You decide to stroll around Webstown. You start walking around town and listening. Just listening.

The same people are still saying the same nice things about your Fixin' shop. You stop by the Sheriff and he still likes you just as much, if not more. It seems everything should be good. The Sheriff still thinks you are the #1 Fixer in Webstown. You walk into a saloon that you missed. As you wander around town you hear whispers.

People are whispering and staring at you. You think about going back and getting your six-shooter. How could this be happening? Why are people pointing and whispering? You run out, and in a hurry take a turn down a side street that often seemed too dark for you. As you walk down this dirty old side street, you notice another store you have never seen before. This store looks like it has been there a long time, respectable. You walk in and realize it's a Complaint Parlor. You walk over to a table with your name on it and see Mia R. signed right next to your face. It reads, "Worse Fixin' Ever". Another in the same handwriting by a Sue F., "I can't believe this person calls that Fixin". Then you realize everyone has been whispering about this.

You are RUINED.

No, you are not ruined. You can talk to the Complaint Parlor Proprietor. You can also go address the entire crowd. It is going to take some time and some work, but you can get everyone talking nicely about you and Your Fixin' Store once again. If not, you can be sure to have enough friends speak highly of you, so that the good comments outweigh the bad.

It could have been worse. If you had not paid attention, it could have destroyed your business. At least you caught the bad mouthing before it got too bad. I have seen lots of Great Stores close up in Webstown and other locales because they paid no attention to these Parlors and similar places. If you had not placed all of those signs, and asked all of those people to say nice things about you, the only things people would have heard out there would have been bad. It could have been the end of The Fabulous Fixer.

With a little work you got all of the bad things taken out of the Complaints Parlor. You even address Mia (who did pretend to be two people) and got things to work again. The extra work you did to get all of those new places talking about you has improved your Fixin' Shop. It's even past where it was in sales before this all started!

So you are good to go!

Hold Your Horses!!! It's not over yet. Another Fixin' shop opened up right next-door. Webstown is growing and changing, and your Fixin' Shop is too busy with current clients for you to continue to build your presence in Webstown. You need help to continue to build your presence and to keep things up and running. This is a good problem to have.

Ok, now for the technical "moral" of the story.

Introduction

The internet is still the wild west because search engines are far from perfect. Search is what allows us to navigate the exponentially growing amount of information. Search with a capital S means the technology behind search engines. With Search currently at about 15% of its full capabilities and social media still in its toddlerhood, there is a lot of room for businesses to grow on the web. I know these numbers are hard to believe, but we are still at the very early stages of this information revolution. Wait until the generation that grew up with Facebook and Google starts running the world. In the time it took me to write this book, there have been about 10 mini revolutions, gold rushes, if you will.

Do you remember the true story of the American Wild West? The frontier was filled with prospectors, oilmen, cowboys, preachers, natives, gold miners, gamblers, developers, and sheriffs. There was huge opportunity as the land was being settled. The late 19th century produced some of the wealthiest people in the history of the world. It also ruined many men.

Many fortunes are yet to be made on the internet. Even if you don't want to run an internet-based business, huge opportunities for your current real world business. This is especially true if you are a fixer, or someone in a service based industry. Whether you fix teeth, legal problems, bodies, or cars, by developing your claim on the web, you can not only find more clients and patients, you can get in touch with a higher quality of client or patient, and you can improve your average sales. You can work less and enjoy what you do more by using the internet to evolve your business.

The Wild West frontier, like the internet, was filled with opportunity and perils. The internet also poses peril for businesses. In any new frontier, there are supposed experts making wild claims out there. Snake oil SEO people will take your money and disappear. The barrier to entry into internet development and marketing is low, so it attracts all types. Add in the anonymity factor, and the result is a cesspool of "black hat" swindlers in the race for your hard earned money. Some don't know what they are doing while others take shortcuts. "Black Hat" is actually the industry SEO (Search Engine Optimization) term for practices that violate Google's (AKA "The Sheriff's") policies. This book will teach you what is truly important on the web to stake your claim so that you can succeed in this awesome frontier and not got tricked by these black hat frauds..

Everything is developing at a breakneck pace, which leads to opportunities. I believe to be able to teach this stuff, you need to be working in it every day. That is why I continue to do hands-on work on a daily basis. I pay attention to the traffic on hundreds of sites and thousands of keywords. I am constantly tweaking and adapting our approach for our clients at authenticWEB. I also listen to my clients to see what is giving them real life success. I love helping small businesses succeed through the internet, because when I help a small business, I am directly helping a real person.

To get started you have to understand what your internet capital is and how to develop it in the right places and in the right way. While many things are changing, these four pieces of internet capital: your domain name, your content, your links, and your online reputation are compulsories that will not be changing anytime soon. That is why I dedicated an entire book to these. The great news is that your internet capital is an investment and, if done properly, will develop over time.

You know about the 80/20 rule. 80% of your results come from 20% of your work. Your internet capital will be the 20% leading to the 80% of the results. **No matter where you are in the growth of your business, this book is for you.**

Even better, your internet capital can be re-purposed later on if you decide to make a move to another industry. No matter where you go and what you do in your life, your capital will be of use to you. You just need a guide on how to do this in an easy and highly effective way.

I am here to be your guide. I have been a guide to those with some knowledge of these roads and those with nothing but a dream to build up their own towns around their business of fixing things. It's not rocket science (although there is some science involved). You just need a good foundation and to understand the Four Pieces of Capital you need to invest in the new frontier. You need to know how to stake your claim on a good foundation and someone to show you what's important and what to avoid.

I have worked as a service professional in finance, real estate, and hospitality in New York City and Orlando, Florida for the last 17 years. I took my first computer programming class when I was 6 years old. I have always enjoyed the digital arts as well as business. I really found my sweet spot when I transitioned into internet marketing through website and search engine optimization, helping lawyers, dentists, doctors, photographers, and other service based professionals win in the Wild West of the Web.

As I said, there are some basic but extremely important things that you, as well as everyone else, need to do. I have explained this to many people. I found that often there is too much noise and others have had trouble understanding these concepts. I wrote the Stake Your Claim story to illustrate how simple it is to lay a good foundation on the internet. **You just need to think of it in basic terms. Don't worry about technology for now.**

GLOSSARY

Before we move on, here is a short glossary, which I think will help you understand some key terms that I will refer to throughout the rest of the book.

Search

Search with a capital S is the technology that organizes information and enables users to find answers. Google wants search to have the perfect answer for everything and everyone, from "What is the best restaurant?" or "What can I do to make my teeth look better?" to "What should I do if I have been in an accident?" or even "What makes the world go around?"

Organic Search Results

These are search results that are given purely on the basis of a complex mathematical formula, an algorithm. This means that there is no manipulation based on the search engine creator's personal objectives. However, there is the combination of traditional Search and Social Media to make search results personal to the individual searcher, also known as "Social Search."

SEO

I am going to refer to SEO often. SEO stands for Search Engine Optimization. Simply put, SEO is making sure that your website(s) are telling the search engines to display your site when people are searching for specific topics. SEO will help you:

- Get to the top of the "organic results" without paying for sponsored results.
- Supply unique opportunities to engage current clients.
- Give you a platform for low cost testing of new services or adjustments to current services.
- Give you the power to make what you want visible to those searching the web.

As long as there is an internet, SEO will always be changing. That is what I love about it! In change there is vast opportunity for business owners just like you.

SEM

SEM or Search Engine Marketing is the practice of marketing your business with paid results by using Search Engines. The entirety of Google's billion dollar empire is based on businesses being in these results. I am not saying this form of marketing does not work. It works very well in some instances. What I am saying is that there are better opportunities to have a much higher return on your investment.

SEM is advertising, and what we are talking about in this book is moving beyond the advertising mentality. SEM can bridge the gap until you have a robust web presence. With SEM you pay for clicks or visibility, usually the former. SEM is advertising that stops once you stop paying, whether for more clicks or a duration of time and will never intermingle with the organic search results. Search engine marketing is a limited-time event. Just like a TV commercial, once it is broadcast, it's over.

Traditional SEO

Traditional SEO is based on the old yellow pages mentality and is combined with a level of commoditization. Someone needs something; they type it into the search engine. I need a new TV, so I type in the kind of TV and find the best price. I need a new car, same thing. Now I need a cosmetic dentist, so I type in cosmetic dentist and start to compare. I need a divorce attorney, same thing. However, as a fixer who cares about your job, you know that EVERY service professional is different. Each professional does things in their own way. Also, the buying cycle for services is different. It's too easy not to do research ahead of time, but focusing solely on traditional SEO for your business results in many missed communication opportunities. People can and will do more research into what they need and whom they want to fulfill that need.

Commoditization

Using traditional SEO practices leads to commoditization. Commoditization is the practice of lowering prices to compete with other businesses. The amount of business you generate starts to depend on how much you charge. Battling on price sucks, especially for talented dentists, lawyers, photographers, contractors, etc. No one wins when a service professional is giving bottom dollar for their valuable knowledge and efforts. Even the consumer does not win, because they are encouraging the person they hire to work for less, which means the fixer needs to work more to make up for that lost income. Commoditization leads to poorer quality fixing.

Service SEO

This is a term I coined because you want to be optimized for the questions people ask about your business. With service SEO you optimize search results to provide your business as the best answer for searchers' questions. Examples include:

- "What should I do if I have been indicted?"
- "Is my child too young for braces?"
- "What is the best legal structure for my going business?"
- "What should I do about my old pipes?"
- "What should I do if I think my husband is cheating?"

By giving the answers to those questions on your website, in video format, and on social media, you are optimizing your content for YOUR service. You are there when people really need your services, instead of just being in their face all the time.

Service SEO:

- Increases your Authority
- Increases the visibility of your business
- Increases the value of your services
- Distinguishes you from others on web
- Decreases closing time
- Converts people that might not even know they need your help

If those are not good enough reasons to optimize for the web, I will give you one more. Service SEO actually helps you get ranked higher for traditional SEO searches, like "Cosmetic Dentist Orlando Fl," or "Personal Injury Attorney New York City, NY."

Four Keys to Winning in the Wild Frontier: Your Internet Capital

To stake your claim and achieve the success offered by the Wild West of the Web, you have to understand what has value to you and what does not, otherwise you can lose time and money searching for fool's gold. Because of the way the internet works and, more importantly, Search, you have the opportunity to claim, settle, and develop your own business in the Wild West of the Web, no matter what you fix. With changing search habits, SEO has created an incredible opportunity for service based businesses to grow at a relatively small cost when compared to traditional marketing and investments. Even better, these investments don't evaporate like traditional media, but actually increase in value over time.

Your internet capital will increase in value as you invest in it. There are four pieces of internet capital you have to develop, maintain, and protect just like "real" capital.

The Four Pieces of Internet Capital are:

1. **Your Domain Names and URLs** [Your claim]

2. **Your Links** [People pointing to your business/Referrals]

3. **Your Content** [The rooms in your fixing shop]

4. **Your Online Reputation** [The talk of the town]

Your First Piece of Internet Capital: Survey and Stake Your Claim

DECIDING ON THE DOMAIN NAME FOR YOUR BUSINESS IS A BIG DEAL!

Own Your Land, Don't Rent

First of all, you should own at least one domain name. I am talking about actually owning the DOMAIN, not just Facebook.com/yourname or yourname.blogspot.com. Although it might be your name and your info on that Facebook page, you do not OWN that address. You are just renting it. Anytime the wealthy landlord, Facebook, Google, Tumblr or Squidoo, decides to change the rules of your land, you are at the whim of whoever owns that domain.

Choosing a Domain Name

Important Domain Details to Improve Search:

Links: The number and quality of links to your domain and any given page (a specific URL). Your links are another piece of your internet capital.

Relative Terms: If you are an dentist, having the word dentists or dentistry in your domain helps in your ranking so dentiststudio.com is better than DrZacharyHodgins.com. This is the same with every other profession.

Details that are Not Important for Improving Search:

.coms: People often ask if they need a .com. People often use .coms as a go-to because they are easy to remember, but they have no weight in search engine ranking.

Multiple Domain Names: Many internet newbies register ten domain names thinking that the keywords will help. The only domain name that matters is the one the site actually exists on. So, if you have BestAttorney.com pointing to Yourlawfirm.com, there is no SEO value..

What should your domain name be?

As we discussed before, Google does consider tAs we discussed before, Google does consider the address of your site in the index. So, if you are an attorney, including "Lawyer" or "Law Firm" in the name will yield better search results. E.g., if both sites are exactly the same, JohnDoeLawFirm.com will come up more often than JohnDoe.com. It might not be as pretty, but it is a better address in Google's eyes. Also, with the previous name it's much easier for people to know what you do if you email them or give them the website, which is an added marketing bonus. However, if you decide on a domain name that is too specific, like OrlandoVeneersdentist.com or OrlandoVillageCrownReplacements.net, you could preclude your business from growing. You can always redirect a domain to a new one later, which will be discussed in a few pages. It's best to get one domain for the near future.

How long should it be?

Brevity is important for many reasons. You want to make it easy for people to remember what your website is and to spell it easily. When I first started our company we were evolvealoud.com. It made sense to me. It made no sense to anyone on the phone. I recommend for you to call someone up and ask them to write down your domain name idea and email it to you. If there is any effort, I would scrap it and go back to your list of potential domain names.

.Com, .Net, .What???

As mentioned, many new businesses want .coms, but they don't carry too much weight for search engines. However, I would suggest avoiding .co's as your primary domain. They can be confusing to type for email purposes or for going directly to a site, because many people type .com automatically.

Are you planning on making the business bigger than just you?

Having YourName.com is a good way to start, like IanGarlic.com. Are you planning on growing? Do you plan on having other consultants, dentists, lawyers, or any other type of fixer working for you and running the show? Do you plan on selling the business one day? These questions should all be taken into consideration because switching domains is not an easy proposition.

Your Second Piece of Internet Capital: Links

Links, Links, Links:

Repeat that mantra. Link, Links, Links. One more time. Links!

Many people do not understand how the Google organic search rankings work. I've heard many people think they are paid rankings. You can not pay Google for higher rankings, nor will anyone at Google adjust the algorithm specifically in favor of one site or another. Google dinged Google Japan for manipulating the search results. They did the same to companies like BMW and JCPenney, both of whom spent millions advertising on Google PPC.

Many think more traffic equals higher rankings. Many people think it's keywords. While these factors might carry a small amount of weight, links hold the most weight in search rankings, specifically inbound links to your site. If you did nothing else but get links, your site would rise in rankings.

It's not what you know; it's who you know. The same goes for the Web. Service professionals always tell me, "I get all of my business from referrals." My first response is, "That's because your website stinks." Because if you are not getting any business from the web, your web presence is not good. The web has officially overcome referrals as the place to find attorneys, according to the ABA Journal.

My second response to that statement goes like this: Google is all about referrals. Referrals at their essence are votes of confidence. On the internet, votes of confidence come in the form of links. Links to your website and within your website tell Google that you are connected in the World Wide Web. Just like with real world referrals, links should be earned through connection and great answers.

Links are now one of the most important factors of your website's ranking in search engines and subsequent traffic. Links made Google a successful search engine. It was the first popular search engine to count in links when deciding ranking, leading to better search results. Links are how one page aims and refers to another. There are many types of links, which I will go over briefly after a quick review of how they work.

Inbound Links

A link to your site is called an inbound link or backlink. These are the links that add value to your website. Inbound links mean links from another website to your website. An inbound link to your site guides a user or a program (another search engine, your browser, or an application) to a specific page from another website. Sometimes it is in the form of an image, like a button, but they are most often a word or phrase like "Click here to download."

By receiving a link from another site (Site A to yours: yourname.com), anyone that visits Site A and clicks on the link to yours will have the opportunity to visit yourname.com, thus increasing traffic. While this is beneficial for generating referral traffic, this is not the main importance of inbound links. Inbound links signal to search engines the authority and topic of your site.

High Quality and High Quantity Links

The number of links pointing to your domain and a specific page is important. This is why I stress having one set domain name vs multiple domain names. Imagine you built up a reputation as Joe Attorney and then changed your name to Joseph Lawyer. While very similar and still you, your reputation would lose authority. It the same thing with having multiple domains.

All of the signs in the town and everyone you know should be pointing to the same domain with their links. They are referring to your site. They can be pointing to different places on the domain, but you don't want to give out 20 web addresses and disperse that authority.

Link Juice or Google Juice, the affectionate term used by SEO professionals, refers to the power of a link in helping your site's ranking in Google.

The amount of link juice a link contains is impacted by several factors including:

- The rank of the page the link came from.
- The age of the link.
- The anchor text.
- The number of links on the page.
- The type of website the link is on.
- Whether or not the link is contextual or part of other text, such as a paragraph.

These are just some of the qualities you have to pay attention to when getting and giving links.

Stop Right There!

Don't Listen to the Guys in Black Hats.

I know what you are thinking. You can put down this book, write some content, and start getting links all over the place. You can beat Google at its own game! Don't do it.

Remember those guys saying they know Google? Remember those guys trying to sell you links? Be very careful here. Violating Google's rules can get your website's rank taken away or worse, get it banned from the search engines. As a rule, don't buy links and don't try shortcuts.

You will get caught if you try shortcuts. Your domain and business will pay the penalty. Just read the New York Times Article about Google and JCPenney. JCPenney spends millions of dollars each year advertising on Google. Still, when the New York Times broke a story about JCPenney buying links, Google lowered JCPenney's ranking.

I am assuming you don't spend millions with Google and do not have the clout of JCPenney, so what makes you think you can game the system? You will eventually get caught, so don't do it. The most recent changes to Google have started to penalize for excessive, unnatural linking. I have seen powerful sites disappear from the Google index.

While there are short term shortcuts in the Wild West of the Web, eventually the Sheriff will catch on and shut you down.

Beware the Black Hats

Doing things like this are referred to as "Black Hat" SEO. While the proponents of it are most likely not going to be wearing black hats or sporting pencil thin mustaches, they may show you fast results and take your money. It will not help in the long run, and black hats will hurt your website.

Be Authentic

Maintaining authenticity becomes important here. You might naturally change who you are and your business will evolve, BUT if you are doing everything in an authentic manner along the way, you will be safe. What do I mean by authentic manner? It's easy. If you would be embarrassed to tell your clients or Google about it, don't do it. Being authentic means operating on the web like you would in real life, as a professional. Be yourself and live your story. To learn more about authenticity, developing it, and it's power, make sure to sign up for our authenticACTION newsletter at authenticACTION.net.

Most likely, if you are reading this book, you do not have the knowledge or time to sustain a black hat or even grey hat SEO campaign. Don't waste your time trying to do so. The short term gains are not worth the possibility of having a condemned sign slapped on your virtual business address. Still, you always want to be building up links to your domain. You can do this while developing your other two pieces of capital, your online reputation and your content.

So how do you build links?

You build links just like you build a real life network. Provide great service, meet like minded people, and help them out. Provide highly valuable information in your own authentic way. It's really that simple. You just learn to do these things online and do them consistently.

Your Third Piece of Internet Capital: Your Content

Building an Empire "One Room at a Time."

You may have heard content is king. Well, that is truth. Content is also your capital. Think of content as the building blocks for your internet empire, the materials and the various rooms or departments for your fixin' shop.

Authentic content creates authority to the Sheriff, i.e. Google. Content answers questions. Content will tell your story, develop your domain, and draw those links. Develop authentic content on your domain to continue to develop your claim.

What is Content?

Content is anything that you put on the web. An article is content. An instant message, an email, a blog post, a photo, an audio file, and a video are all types of content. When people search the web, they are searching for answers. Any form that answer takes is content.

As a business owner, you want most of the needed content to be on your site so that it will lead new clients to you. At the very worst, more content will lead to better visibility for your business.

Build on Your Own Property.

Ask yourself this: Would you redecorate your rented office? Probably. Would you gut renovate that leased apartment? Probably not. When you spend a lot of time writing paragraph upon paragraph, page upon page, it is like gut renovation. Do you really want to do that on someone else's property?

Creating a two minute informational movie or an audio piece is the same thing. Where should you put these things? On YOUR domain, your website. Develop your claim with content. Do not put huge paragraphs on Facebook. Do not put all of your best movies on YouTube. Control your content.

There are reasons to develop content in other places, but you want that content to lead back to your site. You want your site on your domain to be the authoritative place for your content, whether written, video, audio, or even great graphics.

Content Draws Links

People talk about great ideas and refer to great ways to fix things. The same thing goes for content in your domain. When you create compelling content, other sites will link to it. Now you are developing your domains with both links and content.

What is good content? Good Content is Authentic.

Ideally, you create content as identifiable as your fingerprint. Authenticity comes into play here. Having a single story about you, how you do business, and why you do business creates authentic content. Your voice and the "why" of what you do improves your content's authenticity. If you are developing large amounts of content, you are going to have a hard time keeping multiple stories straight for yourself. Trying to be everything to everyone leads to generic, boring content. Authentic content contains your message and your point of view. Wikipedia contains "just the facts" (most of the time) and anyone can go there. Give your content its own spin.

How do you want people to remember your business? People do not describe you through your resume. You have unique identifying characteristics, your Authentic Story.

What to write?

"You never get Talker's Block." – Seth Godin

Everyday the business climate changes. You have new experiences and the world around you develops. All of these experiences provide you fodder. Start to keep notes of the questions clients ask you. Pay attention to relevant news stories. Listen to the stories around you. All are potential content for your domain.

There are many other techniques and ways to develop your content. Make sure to subscribe to our authenticWEB newsletter for content ideas.

You never know who is going to need that room in your House of Fixing

Think of each piece of content as a room in your virtual office where you help a specific problem. A piece of content can lie dormant. It may be that no one will walk through that door for years, but then one day someone might ask that very specific question, walk through the door, and find you as the authority because you help with their very specific problem. You then have a new client!

Content builds your own links

Remember the importance of links. Internal links refer to other content on your own website, and Google does index them so that internal content becomes more important. The more you link to an internal page on your site, the more power that page has.

Content draws attention and links

If you take the time to create great content, people will link to it. Just like you probably refer to newspaper articles in normal speech, online writers may link to your content. The content does need to be exceptional. In what way can you improve your chances of getting that link? Write more content consistently. The more you write and respond to the world around you, the more you will improve and draw the attention of links.

Consistently develop your claim

Hopefully at this point you see how we are developing links and content at the same time. While the results may not be immediate, with consistent work on these pieces of capital, on your piece of land, your business success will grow on the web.

Now for the last piece of capital, which is what others are actually saying about you on the web, i.e. your online reputation.

Your Fourth Piece of Capital in the Virtual Frontier: Your Online Reputation

Many business owners do not take the time to go past the first page of search results when looking for their name. Like taking a walk around town to hear about your business from others, you need to actively monitor your online reputation.

Online Reputation

It used to be your reputation drew its meaning from your real life actions and your personal circle of friends, family, and acquaintances. It was not imperative to monitor your reputation unless it was really good or really bad. Few ways to actively monitor your reputation were available. The internet changed that. Now you have to monitor your online reputation. How often have you Googled a business before doing anything else? Probably every time.

How many old classmates have you looked for on Facebook? How many pictures have you perused? Eighty percent of companies are using Linkedin as their major hiring tool. People are looking for you and using many different tools on the internet. Usually though, the search for you starts with Google.

Beyond simply monitoring, you need to be proactive by developing content about you and taking hold of your online persona. There will come a time when, no matter how good of a job you do in real life, your online reputation will come into play. Monitoring it and being proactive will keep your business and your bottom line from suffering.

A Brave New World

I am still assuming you are doing the best job possible and trying to listen to your clients and respond to their needs. No matter what you do, you will encounter difficult clients, unreasonable clients, and certifiably crazy clients. We all have those clients that, no matter what you do, they erupt over and over again. You know who they are. You see and hear their rants, and, most likely those around them take all of their complaints with a grain of salt. But the internet enables a new kind of complainer, an anonymous one that can destroy your business.

There is also another type of person that, up until a few years ago, would keep their mouth shut. They do not return faulty items to a store, and they will not complain about poor service at your restaurant. They will just simmer and smile. Either of these people's comments can affect your online reputation.

You might not find their comments if you are not looking.

Often business owners focus on building their business and ignore their online reputation. New internet marketers pay attention to who is #1 in Google for their industry. They don't pay attention to their online reputation until it is too late. All of a sudden they will notice a dip in their business with no discernible reason. The site still ranks, traffic did not change, their advertising has not changed, and everyone in the office seems just as happy. However, overall business has gone to the pooper.

It could be that you are not paying attention to your online reputation. Regularly doing searches for your business name and your name helps to prevent a major problem. One way to do this is Google alerts. It's easy to set up for a variety of search terms, and it will alert you to any new things that show up in the search engine's quest for that term, such as a Google Alert for your name.

Be active throughout the rest of the Web.

Online Reputation Management Builds the Rest of Your Online Capital

I know I told you to develop your presence on your domain, but that does not mean you should ignore the rest of the web. By being active on other sites like Facebook, Linkedin, and Yelp, you can distribute content and develop other content on those sites. Just don't spend the majority of your time there.

Monitoring your online reputation and proactively developing it will naturally put you in a position to create more content. That content being distributed will naturally build more links. Building more links will increase the authority of your domain and your content, which will help your online reputation. An improved online reputation will improve your bottom line. It"s a pretty nifty pattern of improvement. With a good online reputation your claim will become a thriving business!

Marketing on the web is not a one time event, however it does not have to be all consuming. By understanding the techniques discussed in this book, you can lay a good foundation. However, you will need to stay on top of your web presence. Success breeds imitators. In order to keep succeeding, you will need to utilize the latest and greatest techniques to stay ahead of the game, but they should all be applied to your domain, increasing your content's quality and quantity, increasing links to your site, and improving your online reputation.

Where to go from here?

Do it yourself

Whether you want to continue to do it yourself or hire someone, subscribe to the authenticACTION weekly update at authenticACTION.net. Also, stay on my mailing list for my latest books, videos, and workshops. I believe in giving subscribers quick to-do items, all of which are based on the philosophies of this book.

Train your staff to do it

At authenticWEB, we only work with small to mid-sized professional companies. I find that you can greatly benefit when you leverage your entire staff, if you have above forty people working for you. I often go in and train a company with an in-house marketing staff. Teaching them the basics and getting them involved will also make it more fun!

Get it all done for you

If you are a professional business offering services, looking to dominate the web, and want someone else to do it, our team at authenticWEB is here to help. We have a unique process to build up all of your pieces of capital and harness your authenticity. We combine website development on the Wordpress platform, Social Media, SEO, Online Video, and Inbound Marketing to make businesses grow and evolve. Call us today for a free consultation. If we can't do it for you, we can point you in the right direction.

The End

"Actually, it's just the beginning..."

Now you have it. Your guide for moving to the Wild West of the Web and staking your claim. It's only the beginning, and there is still a lot to do if you want to really strike it rich, but you now have the foundation. With this foundation, you now know how to prevent yourself from getting swindled.

You also now know where to spend your time and efforts initially. First, sign up for a great domain name and use only one for now. Do all of your development there. Then start to build a variety of content for your domain. Building great content creates many rooms for your fixing services. This content should discuss every single problem in the realms of your service that is possible. If you did nothing else but build content, ORIGINAL and AUTHENTIC content, you would do well. It would take a lot more content though, if you did not do the rest of the things we talked about in Stake Your Claim.

Next, make sure you are building links. Links are the referrals to you and your content, the signs and doorways to your many rooms. Do not try to pay people off for the links, and make sure you are not upsetting the Sheriff. Get links in the same way you ask for referrals. It should be a natural process.

Finally, manage your online reputation. It's easy to ignore your online reputation, but it will undermine your entire operation. Pay attention to what people are saying and actively get out there to spread the word about your business.

Improve all four pieces of your internet capital and you will continue to improve your claim. I bet you came here to do better than ok though. You will want to make your store prettier (web design). For this, you will need to gather advice by hiring consultants like the one that brought you out here. Eventually you will not have time to do all of the work. It will then be time to hire an agency, like authenticWEB, and move from being a store on the frontier to a powerhouse business dominating the town.

Whatever your next step may be, go over to authenticWEB.com and sign up for our authenticACTION newsletter, which will keep you up to date on the latest ways to win in the Wild West of the Web.

Good luck, and I'll see y'all soon!!

About Ian Garlic and authenticWEB

Ian Garlic is a born entrepreneur and has worked in many industries. He has been the marketing adviser to hundreds of law firms and small businesses, as well as consultant to several fortune 500 companies and global organizations.

He has a passion for helping others succeed, and loves to inspire others to new heights. Ian creates films, runs barefoot on trails, makes unique meals for friends and family, and talks about business the rest of the time.

authenticWEB is a world class inbound marketing agency founded by Ian Garlic and Jessica Curry Garlic. The team at authenticWEB helps small businesses to thrive through their stories. They do this through award winning SEO services, Website Design, Online Video Production, and Marketing Automation with Infusionsoft. They offer a free initial consultation.

yourauthenticweb.com